Table of Con

Changing Places

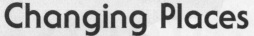

You run to catch the school bus. The bus rolls down the road. Tree branches sway in the breeze. An airplane flies up into the sky.

AMAZING SCIENCE

Motion

Push and Pull, Fast and Slow

Written by Darlene R. Stille
Illustrated by Sheree Boyd

Special thanks to our advisers for their expertise:

Paul Ohmann, Ph.D., Assistant Professor of Physics
University of St. Thomas, St. Paul, Minnesota

Susan Kesselring, M.A., Literacy Educator
Rosemount-Apple Valley-Eagan (Minnesota) School District

PICTURE WINDOW BOOKS
a capstone imprint

Managing Editor: Bob Temple
Creative Director: Terri Foley
Editor: Nadia Higgins
Editorial Adviser: Andrea Cascardi
Copy Editor: Laurie Kahn
Designer: John Moldstad
Page production: Picture Window Books
The illustrations in this book were prepared digitally.

Picture Window Books
A Capstone Imprint
1710 Roe Crest Drive
North Mankato, MN 56003
www.capstonepub.com

Library of Congress Cataloging-in-Publication Data
Stille, Darlene R.
Motion : push and pull, fast and slow / written by Darlene Stille ;
illustrated by Sheree Boyd.
p. cm. — (Amazing science)
Includes bibliographical references and index.
Contents: Changing places—How things move—Let's get going!—
Who's moving?— Experiments—Fun facts.
ISBN 978-1-4048-0250-6 (hardcover)
ISBN 978-1-4048-0348-0 (paperback)
ISBN 978-1-4795-5172-9 (saddle stitch)
1. Motion—Juvenile literature. 2. Force and energy—Juvenile literature.
[1. Motion. 2. Force and energy.]
I. Boyd, Sheree ill. II. Title. III. Series.
QC133.5.S75 2004
531'.11—dc22
2003016463

Printed in China by Nordica
0913/CA21301712
072013   007632

Anything that goes from one place to another is in motion.

FUN FACT

There are all kinds of words to describe motion. You can run, walk, jump, dance, swim, slide, and skate. Birds soar. Snakes slither. Monkeys swing from tree to tree. What other motion words can you think of?

How Things Move
Up and down. Forward and backward.
Some things move in straight lines.

6

Sideways or around and around.
Some things move in curved lines.

A car whizzes down the road.
A baseball crashes through a window.
Some things move quickly.

FUN FACT

How fast something moves is called its speed. You can measure speed. When the needle on a car speedometer points to 60, it means that it will take one hour for the car to move 60 miles (97 kilometers).

A baby crawls across a room. A ball of yarn unwinds and rolls away. Some things move slowly.

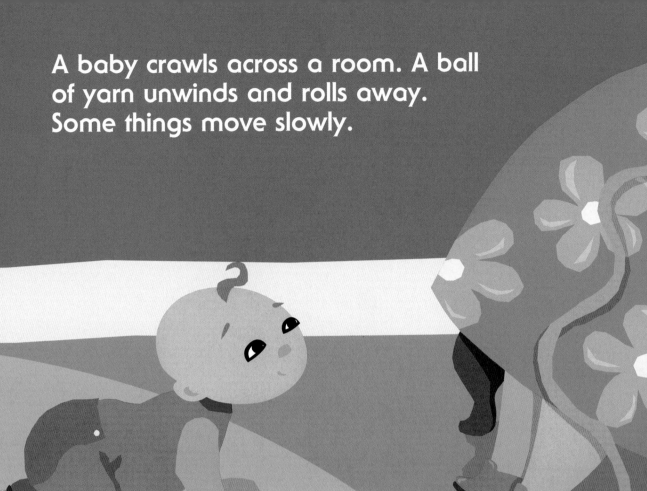

Let's Get Going!

A kick from your foot makes the ball scoot across the field. Stepping on the gas pedal makes the car drive away.

Inertia is a property of all matter. Inertia won't let things move unless a force gets them going. A kick is the force that moves a ball. A motor creates the force that moves a car.

FUN FACT

Pushing down on the car's gas pedal adds force. It makes the car go faster and faster. Going faster and faster is called acceleration.

Your bag slips off your shoulder. What is the force that got it going? What makes yo-yos dip and water spill? Why do baseballs curve down?

The earth's gravity is the force that pulls everything down toward the ground.

FUN FACT

Things speed up as they fall. A raindrop that is close to the ground is falling faster than a raindrop high up in the sky.

A rolling ball, a speeding car, and a falling raindrop will keep moving until something stops them. Inertia also makes moving things keep on moving.

You need to wear a seat belt because of inertia. Suppose your car stops suddenly. Your body will keep moving forward until a force stops it. A seat belt stops your body and keeps you safe.

FUN FACT

Inertia also keeps things moving in one direction. It takes an outside force to turn or spin something. Your bike won't turn unless you move the handlebars. Kites won't dip without wind. A baseball won't curve down without gravity.

The ball you kicked rolls across the grass. As the grass rubs against it, the ball slows down and stops. This rubbing is called friction. Friction is a force that makes things slow down or stop moving.

Anything that rubs can cause friction—even air! People who design airplanes think a lot about how to keep air from slowing things down.

FUN FACT

You need friction to walk from one place to another. Your shoes rub against the ground. This makes friction that keeps you from sliding all over the place.

Who's Moving?

You are on a moving bus. Some friends outside see you looking out the window and wave. Your friends outside think you are moving very fast.

But what about the friend next to you? Does this friend think that you are moving fast? Not at all!

FUN FACT

Think about driving down the highway. The cars in the other lanes don't seem to be moving fast when your car is moving alongside them.

19

The world is full of motion you can't sense. Even as you read this book, you are speeding through space! You are on the earth, and the earth is spinning around and circling the sun.

Leaves are fluttering. Raindrops are falling. Cars are whizzing by. Look for motion and the forces that create it in everything around you.

FUN FACT

It looks like the sun moves across the sky, but that is not the case at all. The earth is moving. As the part of the earth that you are on turns toward the sun, it becomes day. As the same part of the earth turns away, it becomes night.

Experiments

Falling Papers

What you need:
a sheet of notebook paper
a sheet of paper from the same notebook, crumpled into a ball

What you do:
1. Hold the flat sheet out in front of you. Let it drop. How does it fall?
2. Hold the crumpled sheet out in front of you. Let it drop. How does it fall?
3. Drop the two sheets of paper at the same time. Which one lands first?

More air can rub against the flat sheet of paper because the surface is bigger. Can you see what friction from the air is doing to the paper as it drops?

Testing Friction

What you need:
basketball or soccer ball
tape measure or yardstick
masking tape

What you do:
1. Pick a spot on a smooth sidewalk. Stick a piece of masking tape on the sidewalk.
2. Set the ball on the piece of tape. Give it a gentle push. Measure how far the ball rolls, and write down your results.
3. Take the ball indoors, and do this test on carpet. Try to use the same force to push the ball each time. Now do this test on a grassy lawn. Try it at the beach or in a sandbox. Each time, write down how far the ball rolls.

Which surface let the ball roll farthest? Which surface created the most friction?

Facts on the Move

Sound Moves
Sound moves in waves. It moves at different speeds. Sound goes faster through metal and water than it does through air. The speed of sound through air at the surface of the sea is 1,116 feet (340 meters) per second. Sound moves more quickly through hot air.

Slowing Down
Brakes on a car use friction. The brakes rub against the wheels. This rubbing makes the wheels turn more slowly. Slowing down is called deceleration.

Cement and Ice
Different surfaces create different amounts of friction. Cement is rough, and ice is smooth. Cement produces more friction than ice. You can skate on ice. You also can slip more easily on ice. The tires of a car roll along on cement, but they spin around and around on ice.

A Tie
Drop a soccer ball and a tennis ball from a rooftop. Which will land first? For a long time, people used to think heavier things fell faster than lighter things. A famous Italian scientist named Galileo proved this is not true. He said that friction from air makes things fall at different speeds. A feather falls more slowly than a pebble because its flat surface rubs against more air, not because it weighs less. Suppose there were no air friction. The soccer ball and the tennis ball would land at the same time.

A Universal Force
Gravity is the force that makes a pencil drop and a bike roll down a hill. Gravity also keeps things from floating off the surface of the earth. Gravity's pull keeps the Moon circling around Earth and all the planets in orbit around the Sun.

The Fastest Thing
Light moves faster than anything else in the universe. The speed of light is 186,282 miles (299,792 kilometers) per second. That's 10 million times as fast as a car on the highway!

Glossary

acceleration–speeding up
force–anything that causes a change in motion
friction–the rubbing of one surface against another. Friction stops or slows down moving things.
gravity–the force that pulls objects toward the earth's surface
inertia–a property of matter that makes things resist changes in motion
speed–how fast something is moving

24